Treatment of *Brady v. Maryland* Material in United States District and State Courts' Rules, Orders, and Policies

Report to the Advisory Committee on
Criminal Rules of the Judicial Conference
of the United States

Laural L. Hooper, Jennifer E. Marsh, and Brian Yeh

Federal Judicial Center

October 2004

This report was undertaken in furtherance of the Federal Judicial Center's statutory mission to conduct and stimulate research and development for the improvement of judicial administration. The views expressed are those of the authors and not necessarily those of the Federal Judicial Center.

Contents

I. Introduction 1
   A. Background: *Brady*, Rule 16, and Rule 11 1
      1. Brady v. Maryland 1
      2. Federal Rule of Criminal Procedure 16 2
      3. Federal Rule of Criminal Procedure 11 3
      4. American College of Trial Lawyers' proposal 3
      5. Department of Justice's response to the ACTL's proposal 4
   B. Summary of Findings 4
      1. Relevant authorities identified in the U.S. district courts 4
      2. Relevant authorities identified in the state courts 5

II. U.S. District Court Policies for the Treatment of *Brady* Material 6
   A. Research Methods 6
   B. Governing Rules, Orders, and Procedures 7
   C. Definition of *Brady* Material 7
      1. Evidence favorable to the defendant 9
      2. Exculpatory evidence or material 9
   D. Disclosure Requirements 11
      1. Time requirements for disclosure 12
      2. Duration of disclosure requirements 13
   E. Due Diligence Requirements 14
   F. Sanctions for Noncompliance with *Brady* Obligations 14
   G. Declination Procedures 15

III. State Court Policies for the Treatment of *Brady* Material 17
   A. Research Methods 17
   B. Governing Rules, Orders, and Procedures 17
   C. Definition of *Brady* Material 18
      1. Evidence favorable to the defendant 18
      2. Exculpatory evidence or material 19
   D. Disclosure Requirements 20
      1. Types of information required to be disclosed 20
      2. Mandatory disclosure without request 22
      3. Disclosure upon request of defendant 23
      4. Time requirements for disclosure 23
   E. Due Diligence Obligations 27
   F. Sanctions for Noncompliance with *Brady* Obligations 27

I. Introduction

In July 2004, the Judicial Conference Advisory Committee on Criminal Rules asked the Federal Judicial Center to study the local rules of the U.S. district courts, state laws, and state court rules that address the disclosure principles contained in *Brady v. Maryland*.[1] *Brady* requires that prosecutors fully disclose to the accused all exculpatory evidence in their possession. Subsequent Supreme Court decisions have elaborated the *Brady* obligations to include the duty to disclose (1) impeachment evidence,[2] (2) favorable evidence in the absence of a request by the accused,[3] and (3) evidence in the possession of persons or organizations (e.g., the police).[4] This report presents the findings of that research.

The committee's interest is in learning whether federal district courts and state courts have adopted any formal rules or standards that provide prosecutors with specific guidance on discharging their *Brady* obligations. Specifically, the committee wanted to know whether the U.S. district and state courts' relevant authorities (1) codify the *Brady* rule; (2) set any specific time when *Brady* material must be disclosed; or (3) require *Brady* material to be disclosed automatically or only on request. In addition, the Center sought information regarding policies in two areas: (1) due diligence obligations of the government to locate and disclose *Brady* material favorable to the defendant, and (2) sanctions for the government's failure to comply specifically with *Brady* disclosure obligations.

This report has three sections. Section I presents a general introduction to the report, along with a summary of our findings. Section II describes the federal district court local rules, orders, and policies that address *Brady* material, and Section III discusses the treatment of *Brady* material in the state courts' statutes, rules, and policies.

A. Background: *Brady*, Rule 16, and Rule 11

1. *Brady v. Maryland*

In *Brady v. Maryland*, the Supreme Court held "that the suppression by the prosecution of evidence favorable to an accused upon request violates due process where the evidence is material either to guilt or punishment, irrespective of the good faith or bad faith of the prosecution."[5] Subsequent Supreme Court decisions have held that the government has a constitutionally mandated, affirmative duty to disclose exculpatory evidence to the defendant to help ensure the defendant's right to a fair trial under the Fifth and Fourteenth Amendments' Due Process

---

1. 373 U.S. 83 (1963).
2. Giglio v. United States, 405 U.S. 150, 153–54 (1972).
3. United States v. Agurs, 427 U.S. 97, 107 (1976).
4. Kyles v. Whitley, 514 U.S. 419, 437 (1995).
5. 373 U.S. at 87.

Clauses.[6] The Court cited as justification for the disclosure obligation of prosecutors "the special role played by the American prosecutor in the search for truth in criminal trials."[7] The prosecutor serves as "'the representative . . . of a sovereignty . . . whose interest . . . in a criminal prosecution is not that it shall win a case, but that justice shall be done.'"[8]

The *Brady* decision did not define what types of evidence are considered "material" to guilt or punishment, but other decisions have attempted to do so. For example, the standard of "materiality" for undisclosed evidence that would constitute a *Brady* violation has evolved over time from "if the omitted evidence creates a reasonable doubt that did not otherwise exist,"[9] to "if there is a reasonable probability that, had the evidence been disclosed to the defense, the result of the proceeding would have been different,"[10] to "whether in [the undisclosed evidence's] absence [the defendant] received a fair trial, understood as a trial resulting in a verdict worthy of confidence,"[11] to the current standard, "when prejudice to the accused ensues . . . [and where] the nondisclosure [is] so serious that there is a reasonable probability that the suppressed evidence would have produced a different verdict."[12]

2. *Federal Rule of Criminal Procedure 16*

Federal Rule of Criminal Procedure 16 governs discovery and inspection of evidence in federal criminal cases. The Notes of the Advisory Committee to the 1974 Amendments expressly said that in revising Rule 16 "to give greater discovery to both the prosecution and the defense," the committee had "decided not to codify the *Brady* Rule."[13] However, the committee explained, "the requirement that the government disclose documents and tangible objects 'material to the preparation of his defense' underscores the importance of disclosure of evidence favorable to the defendant."[14]

Rule 16 entitles the defendant to receive, upon request, the following information:

- statements made by the defendant;
- the defendant's prior criminal record;

---

6. *See* United States v. Bagley, 473 U.S. 667, 675 (1985) ("The *Brady* rule is based on the requirement of due process. Its purpose is not to displace the adversary system as the primary means by which truth is uncovered, but to ensure that a miscarriage of justice does not occur.").

7. Strickler v. Greene, 527 U.S. 263, 281 (1999).

8. Kyles v. Whitley, 514 U.S. 419, 439 (1995) (*quoting* Berger v. United States, 295 U.S. 78, 88 (1935)).

9. United States v. Agurs, 427 U.S. 97, 112 (1976).

10. *Bagley*, 473 U.S. at 682.

11. *Kyles*, 514 U.S. at 434.

12. *Strickler*, 527 U.S. at 281–82.

13. Fed. R. Crim. P. 16 advisory committee's note (italics added).

14. *Id.*

- documents and tangible objects within the government's possession that "are material to the preparation of the defendant's defense or are intended for use by the government as evidence in chief at the trial, or were obtained from or belong to the defendant";
- reports of examinations and tests that are material to the preparation of the defense; and
- written summaries of expert testimony that the government intends to use during its case in chief at trial.[15]

Rule 16 also imposes on the government a continuing duty to disclose additional evidence or material subject to discovery under the rule, if the government discovers such information prior to or during the trial.[16] Finally, Rule 16 grants the court discretion to issue sanctions or other orders "as are just" in the event the government fails to comply with a discovery request made under the rule.[17]

3. *Federal Rule of Criminal Procedure 11*

Federal Rule of Criminal Procedure 11 governs prosecutor and defendant practices during plea negotiations. The Supreme Court has not said whether disclosure of exculpatory evidence is required in the context of plea negotiations; however, in *United States v. Ruiz*, the Court held that the government is not constitutionally required to disclose *impeachment* evidence to a defendant prior to entering a plea agreement.[18] The Court noted that "impeachment information is special in relation to the *fairness of a trial,* not in respect to whether a plea is *voluntary* ('knowing,' 'intelligent,' and 'sufficiently aware')."[19] The Court stated that "[t]he degree of help that impeachment information can provide will depend upon the defendant's own independent knowledge of the prosecution's potential case—a matter that the Constitution does not require prosecutors to disclose."[20] Finally, the Court stated that "a constitutional obligation to provide impeachment information during plea bargaining, prior to entry of a guilty plea, could seriously interfere with the Government's interest in securing those guilty pleas that are factually justified, desired by defendants, and help to secure the efficient administration of justice."[21]

4. *American College of Trial Lawyers' proposal*

In October 2003, the American College of Trial Lawyers (ACTL) proposed amending Federal Rules of Criminal Procedure 11 and 16 in order to "codify the rule of law first propounded in *Brady v. Maryland*, clarify both the nature and

---

15. Fed. R. Crim. P. 16(a)(1)(A)–(E).
16. Fed. R. Crim. P. 16(c).
17. Fed. R. Crim. P. 16(d)(2).
18. 536 U.S. 622, 633 (2002).
19. *Id.* at 629 (quoting Brady v. United States, 397 U.S. 742, 748 (1970)).
20. *Id.* at 630.
21. *Id.* at 631.

scope of favorable information, require the attorney for the government to exercise due diligence in locating information and establish deadlines by which the United States must disclose favorable information."[22]

5. *Department of Justice's response to the ACTL's proposal*

The Department of Justice (DOJ) opposes the ACTL's proposal to amend Federal Rules of Criminal Procedure 11 and 16. DOJ contends that the government's *Brady* obligations are "clearly defined by existing law that is the product of more than four decades of experience with the *Brady* rule," and therefore no codification of the *Brady* rule is warranted.[23]

B. Summary of Findings

1. *Relevant authorities identified in the U.S. district courts*

- Thirty of the ninety-four districts reported having a relevant local rule, order, or procedure governing disclosure of *Brady* material. References to *Brady* material are usually in the courts' local rules but are sometimes in standard or standing orders and joint discovery statements.
- Eighteen of the thirty districts that explicitly reference *Brady* material use the term "favorable to the defendant" in describing evidence subject to the disclosure obligation. Nine other districts refer to *Brady* material as evidence that is exculpatory in nature. One additional district uses neither term, and two other additional districts use both terms in defining *Brady* material.
- Twenty-one of the thirty districts mandate automatic disclosure; five dictate that the government provide such material only upon request of the defendant. One district requires parties to address *Brady* material in a pretrial conference statement, and three are silent on disclosure.
- The thirty districts that reference *Brady* material vary significantly in their timetables for disclosure of the material. The most common time frame is "within 14 days of the arraignment," followed by "within five days of the arraignment." Some districts have no specified time requirements for disclosure, using terms such as "as soon as reasonably possible" or "before the trial."
- In twenty-two of the thirty districts with *Brady*-related provisions, the disclosure obligation is a continuing one, such that if additional evidence is discovered during the trial or after initial disclosure, the defendant must be notified and provided with the new evidence.

---

22. Memorandum from American College of Trial Lawyers to the Judicial Conference Advisory Committee on Federal Rules of Criminal Procedure (October 2003), at 2.

23. Memorandum from U.S. Department of Justice (Criminal Division) to Hon. Susan C. Bucklew, Chair, Judicial Conference Subcommittee on Rules 11 and 16 (April 26, 2004), at 2.

- Of the thirty districts with policies governing *Brady* material, five have specific due diligence requirements for prosecutors. One district has a certificate of compliance requirement only. The remaining twenty-four districts do not appear to have due diligence requirements.
- None of the districts specify sanctions for nondisclosure by prosecutors, leaving any sanction determination to the discretion of the court.
- Three of the thirty districts that reference *Brady* have declination procedures for disclosure of specific types of information.

2. *Relevant authorities identified in the state courts*

- All fifty states and the District of Columbia have a rule or other type of authority, including statutes, concerning the prosecutor's obligation to disclose information favorable to the defendant.
- Many of the states have enacted rules similar to Federal Rule of Criminal Procedure 16; however, some of these rules and statutes vary in their details. Some states go beyond the scope of Rule 16 and the *Brady* constitutional obligations by explicitly setting time limits on disclosure; other states have adopted Rule 16 almost verbatim, using language like "evidence material to the preparation of the defense" and "evidence favorable to the defendant."
- Most states' rules impose a continuing disclosure obligation, such that if additional evidence is discovered during the trial or after initial disclosure, the defendant must be promptly notified and shown such new evidence.
- A few states have a specific due diligence obligation that requires prosecutors to submit a "certificate of compliance" indicating that they have exercised due diligence in locating favorable evidence and that, to the best of their knowledge and belief, all such information has been disclosed to the defense.
- All of the states authorize sanctions for prosecutors' failure to comply with discovery obligations and other state-court-mandated disclosure requirements. A few states permit a trial court to dismiss charges entirely as a sanction for prosecutorial misconduct, while other states have held dismissal to be too severe a sanction.

II. U.S. District Court Policies for the Treatment of *Brady* Material

In this section, we describe federal local court rules, orders, and procedures in the thirty responding districts that codify the *Brady* rule, define *Brady* material and/or set the timing and conditions for disclosure of *Brady* material. In addition, we discuss due diligence obligations of the government and specific sanctions for the government's failure to comply with disclosure procedures.

A. Research Methods

Because of the short time we had to complete our research, we were unable to survey each district court about compliance with its *Brady* practices, that is, the degree to which the court's rules and other policies describe what actually occurs in the district. To obtain a comprehensive picture of such practices, we would need to survey U.S. attorneys, federal public defenders, and selected retained or appointed defense counsel in each of the ninety-four districts. Such a survey would be considerably more time-consuming than the research conducted for this report.

We searched the Westlaw RULES-ALL and ORDERS-ALL databases using the following search terms:

- "Brady v. Maryland" & ci(usdct!);
- "exculpatory" & ci(usdct!);
- "exculpatory evidence" & ci(usdct!); and
- "evidence favorable to the defendant" & ci(usdct!).

In addition, we reviewed paper copies of each district court's local rules. For twenty-two districts, these database and paper-copy searches yielded specific local rules and orders that relate to the *Brady* decision or that set forth guidance to the government regarding disclosure of *Brady* material. For the seventy-two (94 minus 22) districts for which our searches did not yield a relevant local rule or order, we contacted the clerks of court to request their assistance in locating any local rules, orders, or procedures relating to the application of the *Brady* decision. Through this effort, we identified eight additional districts (for a total of thirty) that clearly refer to *Brady* material in their local rules, orders, or procedures.

We also received responses from another eight districts that do not clearly refer to *Brady* material, but that provided summary information about their disclosure policies.[24] Some districts responded with statements such as "We have not promulgated any local rule and/or general order referencing *Brady* material." Others stated, "We have not adopted any formal standards or rules that provide guidance to prosecutors on discharging *Brady* obligations." And a few districts

---

24. These districts were M.D. La., N.D. Miss., E.D. Mo., W.D.N.Y., N.D. Ohio, M.D. Pa., D.S.C., and D.V.I.

reported, "We follow Federal Rule of Criminal Procedure 16." In most instances, these districts did not provide any other information regarding how *Brady* material disclosures operated in their districts.

The thirty districts that have local rules, orders, and procedures specifically addressing *Brady* material served as the basis for the federal courts section of our analysis. We reviewed and analyzed each of the thirty districts' rules, orders, and published procedures to determine

- the types of information defined as *Brady* material;
- whether the material is disclosed automatically or only upon request;
- the timing of disclosure;
- whether the parties had a continuing duty to disclose;
- whether the parties had a due diligence requirement; and
- whether there are specific provisions authorizing sanctions for failure to disclose *Brady* material.

We also noted whether the districts had declination procedures.

B. Governing Rules, Orders, and Procedures

We found references to *Brady* material in various documents, including local rules, orders (including standing orders and standard discovery, arraignment, scheduling, and pretrial orders), and supplementary materials such as joint statements of discovery and checklists (including disclosure agreement checklists).

Provisions for obligations to disclose *Brady* material are contained in the documents listed in Table 1.[25] We were unable to find information on each of the variables discussed here for all districts. Consequently, this is not a comprehensive description of each of the thirty districts' procedures.

C. Definition of *Brady* Material

Most disclosure rules, orders, and procedures in the thirty districts that address the *Brady* decision define *Brady* material in one of two ways: as evidence favorable to the defendant (18 districts),[26] or as exculpatory evidence (9 districts).[27] One

---

25. Two of the thirty districts (W.D. Okla., D. Vt.) address *Brady*-material disclosure in more than one document.

26. M.D. Ala. Standing Order on Criminal Discovery § (1)(B); S.D. Ala. L.R. 16.13(b)(1)); N.D. Cal. Crim. L.R. 17.1-1(b)(3); D. Conn. L. Crim. R. App. Standing Order on Discovery § (A)(11); N.D. Fla. L.R. 26.3(D)(1); S.D. Fla. L.R. Gen. Rule 88.10; M.D. Ga. Standard Pretrial Order; S.D. Ga. L. Crim. R. 16.1(f); D. Idaho Crim. Proc. Order §§ I(5) & (I)5(a); W.D. Mo. Scheduling and Trial Order § VI.A.; D. Nev. Joint Discovery Statement § II; W.D. Okla. App. 5, § 5; W.D. Pa. L. Crim. R. 16.1(F); E.D. Tenn. Discovery and Scheduling Order (sample); M.D. Tenn. L.R. 10(a)(2)(d); D. Vt. L. Crim. R. 16.1(a)(2); W.D. Wash. Crim. R. 16(a)(1)(K); and S.D. W. Va. Arraignment Order and Standard Discovery Requests § (3)(1)(H)).

27. S.D. Ind. Notification of Assigned Judge, Automatic Not Guilty Plea, Trial Date, Discovery Order, and Other Matters § VII(a)(1)(h); D. Mass. Crim. R. 116.02(A); D.N.H. L. Crim. R.

district (Western District of Kentucky) refers to the material by case name ("*Brady* material") but does not define it further—for example, the terms "evidence favorable to the defendant" or "exculpatory evidence" do not appear in the order.[28] Finally, two districts (Northern District of Georgia[29] and Northern District of New York[30]) use both terms, "evidence favorable to the defendant" and "exculpatory evidence," to define *Brady* material.

Table 1. District Court Documents That Reference *Brady* Material

Documents	Number of Districts	Districts
Local rules	16	S.D. Ala., N.D. Cal., N.D. Fla., S.D. Fla., S.D. Ga., D. Mass., D.N.H., D.N.M., N.D.N.Y., E.D.N.C., W.D. Okla., W.D. Pa., D.R.I., M.D. Tenn., W.D. Wash., E.D. Wis.
Standard orders	3	M.D. Ga., S.D. Ind., D. Vt.
Standing orders	2	M.D. Ala., D. Conn.
Procedural orders	1	D. Idaho
Arraignment orders & standard discovery requests	1	S.D. W.Va.
Arraignment orders & reciprocal orders of discovery	1	W.D. Ky.
Joint discovery statements	2	D. Nev., W.D. Okla.
Discovery & scheduling orders	1	E.D. Tenn.
Scheduling orders	1	W.D. Mo.
Magistrate judges' pretrial orders	1	N.D. Ga.
Criminal pretrial orders	1	D. Vt.
Criminal progression orders	1	D. Neb.
Model checklists	1	W.D. Tex.

16.1(c); D.N.M. L.R.-Crim. R. 16.1; E.D.N.C. L. Crim. R. 16.1(b)(6); D.R.I. R. 12(e); W.D. Tex. Crim. R. 16 (Model Checklist); N.D. W. Va. L.R. Crim. P. 16.05; and E.D. Wis. Crim. L.R. 16.1(b) & (c).

28. W.D. Ky. Arraignment Order & Reciprocal Order of Discovery § (4)(V).

29. N.D. Ga. Magistrate Judge's Pretrial Order § IV(B).

30. N.D.N.Y. L.R. Crim. P. 14.1(b)(2) ("favorable to the defendant"), and N.D.N.Y. L.R. Crim. P. 17.1.1(c) ("exculpatory and other evidence").

1. Evidence favorable to the defendant

The most common definition of "evidence favorable to the defendant," found in ten of the eighteen districts that use the term, defines *Brady* material as any material or information that may be favorable to the defendant on the issues of guilt or punishment and that is within the scope (or meaning) of *Brady*.[31] Three of the ten districts add the qualifier "without regard to materiality."[32]

2. Exculpatory evidence or material

Nine districts refer to *Brady* material as exculpatory in nature.[33] Seven of these use the terms "exculpatory evidence" or "exculpatory material."[34] An eighth district, Rhode Island, refers to "material or information, which tends to negate the guilt of the accused or to reduce his punishment for the offense charged."[35] Finally, the ninth district, New Mexico, specifically provides for an assessment of the material where there is disagreement among the parties: "if a question exists of the exculpatory nature of material sought under *Brady*, it will be made available for in camera inspection at the earliest possible time."[36]

Of these nine districts, Massachusetts has the most detailed and expansive rule dealing with *Brady* material and exculpatory evidence. It defines exculpatory evidence as follows:

- Information that would tend directly to negate the defendant's guilt concerning any count in the indictment or information.

- Information that would cast doubt on the admissibility of evidence that the government anticipates offering in its case-in-chief and that could be subject to a motion to suppress or exclude, which would, if allowed, be appealable under 18 U.S.C. § 3731.

---

31. M.D. Ala. Standing Order on Criminal Discovery § (1)(B); S.D. Ala. L.R. 16.13(b)(1)); D. Conn. L. Crim. R. App. Standing Order on Discovery § (A)(11); N.D. Fla. L.R. 26.3(D)(1); S.D. Fla. L.R. Gen. Rule 88.10; W.D. Mo. Scheduling and Trial Order § VI.A.; E.D. Tenn. Discovery and Scheduling Order (sample); M.D. Tenn. Rule 10(a)(2)(d); D. Vt. L. Crim. R. 16.1(a)(2); and W.D. Wash. Crim. R. 16(a)(1)(K).

32. M.D. Ala. Standing Order on Criminal Discovery § (1)(B); S.D. Ala. L.R. 16.13(b)(1)); and N.D. Fla. L.R. 26.3(D)(1).

33. S.D. Ind. Notification of Assigned Judge, Automatic Not Guilty Plea, Trial Date, Discovery Order, and Other Matters § VII(a)(1)(h); D. Mass. Crim. R. 116.02(A); D.N.H. L. Crim. R. 16.1(c); D.N.M. L.R.-Crim. R. 16.1; E.D.N.C. L. Crim. R. 16.1(b)(6); D.R.I. R. 12(e); W.D. Tex. Crim. R. 16 (Model Checklist); N.D. W. Va. L.R. Crim. P. 16.05; and E.D. Wis. Crim. L.R. 16.1(b) & (c).

34. S.D. Ind. Notification of Assigned Judge, Automatic Not Guilty Plea, Trial Date, Discovery Order, and Other Matters § VII(a)(1)(h); D. Mass. Crim. R. 116.02(A); D.N.H. L. Crim. R. 16.1(c); E.D.N.C. L. Crim. R. 16.1(b)(6); W.D. Tex. Crim. R. 16 (Model Checklist); N.D. W. Va. L.R. Crim. P. 16.05; and E.D. Wis. Crim. L.R. 16.1(b) & (c).

35. D.R.I. R. 12(e).

36. D.N.M. Crim. R. 16.1.

- A statement whether any promise, reward, or inducement has been given to any witness whom the government anticipates calling in its case-in-chief, identifying by name each such witness and each promise, reward, or inducement, and a copy of any promise, reward, or inducement reduced to writing.

- A copy of any criminal record of any witness identified by name whom the government anticipates calling in its case-in-chief.

- A written description of any criminal cases pending against any witness identified by name whom the government anticipates calling in its case-in-chief.

- A written description of the failure of any percipient witness identified by name to make a positive identification of a defendant, if any identification procedure has been held with such a witness with respect to the crime at issue.

- Any information that tends to cast doubt on the credibility or accuracy of any witness whom or evidence that the government anticipates calling or offering in its case-in-chief.

- Any inconsistent statement, or a description of such a statement, made orally or in writing by any witness whom the government anticipates calling in its case-in-chief, regarding the alleged criminal conduct of the defendant.

- Any statement, or a description of such a statement, made orally or in writing by any person, that is inconsistent with any statement made orally or in writing by any witness the government anticipates calling in its case-in-chief, regarding the alleged criminal conduct of the defendant.

- Information reflecting bias or prejudice against the defendant by any witness whom the government anticipates calling in its case-in-chief.

- A written description of any prosecutable federal offense known by the government to have been committed by any witness whom the government anticipates calling in its case-in-chief.

- A written description of any conduct that may be admissible under Fed. R. Evid. 608(b) known by the government to have been committed by a witness whom the government anticipates calling in its case-in-chief.

- Information known to the government of any mental or physical impairment of any witness whom the government anticipates calling in its case-in-chief, that may cast doubt on the ability of that witness to testify accurately or truthfully at trial as to any relevant event.

- Exculpatory information regarding any witness or evidence that the government intends to offer in rebuttal.

- A written summary of any information in the government's possession that tends to diminish the degree of the defendant's culpability or the defendant's Offense Level under the United States Sentencing Guidelines.[37]

---

37. D. Mass. L.R. 116.2(B).

D. Disclosure Requirements

Twenty-one districts mandate automatic disclosure of *Brady* material.[38] One, the Middle District of Georgia, has a caveat—the government need not furnish the defendant with *Brady* information that the defendant has obtained, or with reasonable diligence, could obtain himself or herself.[39] New Mexico mandates "discussion" of disclosure, and says that in camera inspection may be needed.[40]

Five districts dictate that the government provide *Brady* material only upon request of the defendant.[41] The Northern District of California adds qualifying language that requires that the parties address the issue "if pertinent to the case," and in their pretrial conference statement "if a conference is held."[42] Three districts[43] do not mention this issue in their local rules or orders.

Only one district specifically addresses the disposition of the information or evidence once the case has been resolved. The Middle District of Tennessee requires that the information or evidence be returned to the "government or destroyed following the completion of the trial, sentencing of the defendant, or completion of the direct appellate process, whichever occurs last."[44] A party who destroys materials must certify the destruction by letter to the government.

---

38. M.D. Ala. Standing Order on Criminal Discovery § (1)(B); S.D. Ala. L.R. 16.13(b)(1); D. Conn. L. Crim. R. App. Standing Order on Discovery § (A)(11); N.D. Fla. L.R. 26.3(D)(1); S.D. Fla. L.R. Gen. Rule 88.10; M.D. Ga. Standard Pretrial Order; S.D. Ind. Notification of Assigned Judge, Automatic Not Guilty Pleas, Trial Date, Discovery Order and Other Matters § VII(a)(1)(H); D. Mass. Crim. R. 116.2(B); W.D. Mo. Scheduling and Trial Order § VI(A); D. Nev. Joint Discovery Statement § II; D.N.M. L.R.-Crim. R. 16.1; D.N.H. L. Crim. R. 16.1(c); N.D.N.Y. L.R. Crim. P. 14.1(b); W.D. Okla. L. Crim. R. 16.1(b) & App. V. Joint Statement of Discovery Conference § 5; W.D. Pa. L. Crim. R. 16.1(F); D.R.I. Rule 12(e)(A)(5); E.D. Tenn. Discovery & Scheduling Order; M.D. Tenn. L.R. 10(a)(2)(d); D. Vt. L. Crim. R. 16.1(a)(2); N.D. W. Va. L.R. Crim. P. 16.05; and E.D. Wis. Crim. L.R. 16.1(b).

39. M.D. Ga. Standard Pretrial Order, citing United States v. Slocum, 708 F.2d 587, 599 (11th Cir. 1983).

40. D.N.M. L.R.-Crim. R. 16.1.

41. N.D. Ga. Standard Magistrate Judge's Pretrial Order; S.D. Ga. L. Crim. R. 16.1(f); E.D.N.C. L. Crim. R. 16.1(b)(6); W.D. Wash. Crim. R. 16(a)(1)(K); and S.D. W. Va. Arraignment Order and Standard Discovery Request § III(1)(H).

42. N.D. Cal. Crim. L.R. 17.1-1(b).

43. D. Idaho, W.D. Ky., and W.D. Tex.

44. M.D. Tenn. R. 12(k).

1. Time requirements for disclosure[45]

The thirty districts vary significantly in their disclosure timetables. Some districts specify a time by which the prosecution must disclose *Brady* material, while other districts rely upon nonspecific terms such as "timely disclosure" or "as soon as practicable."

a. Specific time requirement

Twenty-five districts have mandated time limits (or specific events, such as hearings or pretrial conferences) for prosecutorial disclosure of *Brady* material (see Table 2).

Table 2. Districts with Time Requirements for Prosecutorial Disclosure of *Brady* Material

Time Requirement	Districts
At arraignment	M.D. Ala.,[46] S.D. Ala.
Within 5 days of arraignment	N.D. Fla., S.D. Ga., W.D. Pa., E.D. Wis.
Within 7 days of arraignment	D. Idaho, N.D. W. Va.
Within 10 days of arraignment	D. Conn., D.R.I., S.D. W. Va.
Within 14 days of arraignment	S.D. Fla., N.D.N.Y., M.D. Tenn., W.D. Tenn., W.D. Tex., D. Vt., W.D. Wash.
Within 28 days of arraignment	D. Mass.
At the discovery conference	W.D. Okla.
Within 10 days of the scheduling order	W.D. Mo.
Prior to the pretrial conference	N.D. Ga.
At the pretrial conference (PTC) (or address in the PTC statement or order)	N.D. Cal., E.D.N.C.
At least 20 days before trial	D.N.H.

---

45. It is well settled that the district court may order when *Brady* material is to be disclosed, United States v. Starusko, 729 F.2d 256 (3d Cir. 1984). Some decisions have held that the Jencks Act controls and that *Brady* material relating to a certain witness need not be disclosed until that witness has testified on direct examination at trial, United States v. Bencs, 28 F.3d 555 (6th Cir. 1994); United States v. Jones, 612 F.2d 453 (9th Cir. 1979); United States v. Scott, 524 F.2d 465 (5th Cir. 1975). Others have held that *Brady* material might be disclosed prior to trial, in order to afford the defendant the opportunity to make effective use of it during trial, United States v. Perez, 870 F.2d 1222 (7th Cir. 1989); United States v. Campagnuolo, 592 F.2d 852 (5th Cir. 1979); United States v. Pollack, 534 F.2d 964 (D.C. Cir. 1976).

46. "or on a date otherwise set by the Court for good cause shown." M.D. Ala. Standing Order on Criminal Discovery § 1.

b. No specific time requirement

Four districts have nonspecific time requirements for disclosure, set out in local rules or in various court orders, or determined by case law.[47] The terms used for these time requirements include the following descriptions:

- "as soon as reasonably possible";[48]
- "before the trial";[49]
- "after defense counsel has entered an appearance";[50] and
- "[t]iming of disclosure should be *described* in the District's standard Arraignment Order/Reciprocal Order of Discovery."[51]

Time requirements for disclosure for one district were not given.[52]

2. *Duration of disclosure requirements*

Twenty-two of the thirty districts make the prosecutor's disclosure obligation a continuing one, such that if additional evidence is discovered during the trial or after initial disclosure, the defendant must be notified and shown the new evidence.[53] A few districts use adjectives or modifiers to more clearly define how soon after discovery of new material the government must disclose it.[54] One dis-

---

47. In the Eastern District of Tennessee, timing of disclosure is governed by *U.S. v. Presser*, 844 F.2d 1275 (6th Cir. 1988), which addressed material that was arguably exempt from pretrial disclosure by the Jencks Act, yet also arguably exculpatory under the *Brady* rule. There, the material needed only to be disclosed to defendants "in time for use at trial."

48. M.D. Ga. Standard Pretrial Order.

49. D. Nev. Joint Discovery Statement § II.

50. S.D. Ind. Notification of Assigned Judge, Automatic Not Guilty Plea, Trial Date, Discovery Order and Other Matters § VII(a)(1)(H).

51. W.D. Ky. Arraignment Order and Reciprocal Order of Discovery § V (emphasis added).

52. D.N.M.

53. M.D. Ala. Standing Order on Criminal Discovery; S.D. Ala. L.R. 16.13(c); D. Conn. L. Crim. R. App. Standing Order on Discovery § D; N.D. Fla. Crim. L.R. 26.3(G); S.D. Fla. L.R. Gen. R. 88.10; S.D. Ga. L. Crim. R. 16.1; D. Idaho Procedural Order § I(5); S.D. Ind. Notification of Assigned Judge, Automatic Not Guilty Plea, Trial Date, Discovery Order and Other Matters § VII(c); W.D. Mo. Scheduling and Trial Order § II; D.N.H. L. Crim. R. 16.2; D.N.M. L.R.-Crim. R. 16.1; N.D.N.Y. L.R. Crim. P. 14.1(f); E.D.N.C. L. Crim. R. 16.1(e); W.D. Okla. App. 5; E.D. Tenn. Discovery and Scheduling Order; M.D. Tenn. R. 10(a)(2); W.D. Tex. C.R. 16(b)(4); D. Vt. L. Crim. R. 16.1(e); W.D. Wash. Crim. R. 16(d); N.D. W. Va. L.R. Crim. P. 16.05; S.D. W. Va. Arraignment Order and Standard Discovery Request § III(4); and E.D. Wis. Crim. L.R. 16(b).

54. *E.g.,* "immediately" (D. Conn. L. Crim. R. App. Standing Order on Discovery § D; S.D. Fla. L.R. Gen. R. 88.10; N.D.N.Y. L.R. Crim. P. 14.1(f); M.D. Tenn. R. 10(a)(2); and N.D. W. Va. L.R. Crim. P. 16.05); "as soon as it is received" (S.D. W. Va. Arraignment Order and Standard Discovery Request § III(4)); "promptly" (S.D. Ind. Notification of Assigned Judge, Automatic Not Guilty Plea, Trial Date, Discovery Order and Other Matters § VII(c); W.D. Tex. C.R. 16(b)(4)); "expeditiously" (M.D. Ala. Standing Order on Criminal Discovery; S.D. Ala. L.R. 16.13(c); N.D.N.Y. L.R. Crim. P. 14.1(f)); and "by the speediest means available" (N.D. Fla. Crim. L.R. 26.3(G)).

trict's local rule explicitly states that motions to enforce the continuing duty "should not be necessary."[55]

E. Due Diligence Requirements

Five districts have specific "due diligence" requirements for prosecutors.[56] Two of these five districts[57] plus one additional district[58] require the government to sign and file a "certificate of compliance" (with *Brady* obligations) with discovery. In one of the five districts, failure to file the certificate of compliance along with a discovery or inspection motion "may result in summary denial of the motion or other sanctions within the discretion of the court."[59]

While other districts do not use the term "due diligence" in their local rules, orders, or procedures, some make it clear that the government has the responsibility to identify and produce discoverable evidence and information. For example, the Western District of Missouri's rule regarding the government's responsibility for reviewing the case file for *Brady* (and *Giglio*) material says:

> The government is advised that if any portion of the government's investigative file or that of any investigating agency is not made available to the defense for inspection, the Court will expect that trial counsel for the government or an attorney under trial counsel's immediate supervision who is familiar with the *Brady/Giglio* doctrine will have reviewed the applicable files for the purpose of ascertaining whether evidence favorable to the defense is contained in the file.[60]

In addition, the Middle and Southern Districts of Alabama include a restriction on the delegation of the responsibility:

> The identification and production of all discoverable information and evidence is the personal responsibility of the Assistant U.S. Attorney assigned to the action and may not be delegated without the express permission of the Court.[61]

F. Sanctions for Noncompliance with *Brady* Obligations

None of the thirty districts specify remedies for prosecutorial nondisclosure. All leave the determination of any sanctions to the discretion of the court.

One district, however, provides some guidance for judges dealing with the failure of the government to comply with *Brady/Giglio* obligations. The Uniform Procedural Order in the District of Idaho says:

---

55. D.N.M. Crim. R. 16.1.
56. D. Conn. L. Crim. R. App. Standing Order on Discovery § A; W.D. Mo. Scheduling and Trial Order § II; D. Nev. Joint Discovery Statement § II; D.N.H. L. Crim. R. 16.2; and W.D. Wash. Crim. R. 16(a).
57. W.D. Mo. and W.D. Wash.
58. D.N.M. *See* D.N.M. L.R.-Crim. R. 16.1. This rule does not use the term "due diligence."
59. W.D. Wash. Crim. R. 16(i).
60. W.D. Mo. Scheduling and Trial Order Note following §§ VI(A) & (B).
61. M.D. Ala. Standing Order on Criminal Discovery; S.D. Ala. L.R. 16.13(b)(2)(C).

> If the government has information in its possession at the time of the arraignment, but elects not to disclose this information until a later time in the proceedings, the court can consider this as one factor in determining whether the defendant can make effective use of the information at trial.[62]

Most courts allow sanctions (generally based on Rule 16's authority) for both parties for general discovery abuses. These sanctions include exclusion of evidence at trial, a finding of contempt, granting of a continuance, and even dismissal of the indictment with prejudice. For example, the Northern District of Georgia's standard Magistrate Judge's Pretrial Order says:

> Where reciprocal discovery is requested by the government, the attorney for the defendant shall personally advise the defendant of the request, the defendant's obligations thereto, and the possibility of sanctions, including exclusion of any such evidence from trial, for failure to comply with the Rule. *See* Fed. R. Crim. P. 16(b) and (d) (as amended December 1, 2002); L.Cr.R. 16.1 (N.D. Ga.).[63]

The Southern District of Florida's Discovery Practices Handbook states that "[i]f a Court order is obtained compelling discovery, unexcused failure to provide a timely response is treated by the Court with the gravity it deserves; willful violation of a Court order is always serious and is treated as contempt."[64] The Northern District of West Virginia's local rule is even more sweeping:

> If at any time during the course of the proceedings it is brought to the attention of the Court that a party has failed to comply with L.R. Crim. P. 16 [the general discovery rule], the Court may order such party to permit the discovery or inspection, grant a continuance or prohibit the party from introducing evidence not disclosed, or the Court may enter such order as it deems just under the circumstances up to and including the dismissal of the indictment with prejudice.[65]

G. Declination Procedures

Three of the thirty districts specifically refer to declination procedures in their local rules or orders.[66] For example, the Southern District of Georgia's local rule says:

> In the event the U.S. Attorney declines to furnish any such information described in this rule, he shall file such declination in writing specifying the types of disclosure

---

62. D. Idaho Uniform Procedural Order § I(5).
63. N.D. Ga. standard Magistrate Judge's Pretrial Order.
64. S.D. Fla. L.R. App. A. Discovery Practices Handbook § I.D(4) Sanctions. Note that the practices set forth in the handbook do not have the force of law, but are for the guidance of practitioners. The *Discovery Practices Handbook* was prepared by the Federal Courts Committee of the Dade County Bar Association and adopted as a published appendix to the Local General Rules.
65. N.D. W. Va. L.R. Crim. P. 16.11.
66. S.D. Ga. L. Crim. R. 16.1(g); D. Mass. L.R. 116.6(A); and W.D. Wash. Crim. R. 16(e).

that are declined and the ground therefor. If defendant's attorney objects to such refusal, he shall move the Court for a hearing therein.[67]

The District of Massachusetts has an even more detailed rule governing the declination of disclosure and protective orders, providing for challenges, sealed filings, and ex parte motions:

> (A) Declination. If in the judgment of a party it would be detrimental to the interests of justice to make any of the disclosures required by these Local Rules, such disclosures may be declined, before or at the time that disclosure is due, and the opposing party advised in writing, with a copy filed in the Clerk's Office, of the specific matters on which disclosure is declined and the reasons for declining. If the opposing party seeks to challenge the declination, that party shall file a motion to compel that states the reasons why disclosure is sought. Upon the filing of such motion, except to the extent otherwise provided by law, the burden shall be on the party declining disclosure to demonstrate, by affidavit and supporting memorandum citing legal authority, why such disclosure should not be made. The declining party may file its submissions in support of declination under seal pursuant to L.R. 7.2 for the Court's in camera consideration. Unless otherwise ordered by the Court, a redacted version of each such submission shall be served on the moving party, which may reply.
>
> (B) Ex Parte Motions for Protective Orders. This Local Rule does not preclude any party from moving under L.R. 7.2 and ex parte (i.e., without serving the opposing party) for leave to file an ex parte motion for a protective order with respect to any discovery matter. Nor does this Local Rule limit the Court's power to accept or reject an ex parte motion or to decide such a motion in any manner it deems appropriate.[68]

Other districts have procedures for motions to deny, modify, restrict, or defer discovery or inspection.[69] The moving party has the burden to show cause why discovery should be limited.

---

67. S.D. Ga. L. Crim. R. 16.1(g). *See also* S.D. Ind. Notification of Assigned Judge, Automatic Not Guilty Plea, Trial Date, Discovery Order and Other Matters (standard order in criminal cases) § VII(d).

68. D. Mass. Crim. R. 116.6. The Western District of Washington has a similar but less detailed and expansive rule. W.D. Wash. Crim. R. 16(e).

69. *See, e.g.,* D. Conn. Standing Order on Discovery § F. The Middle District of Tennessee's standing order language is similar to Connecticut's; however, the Middle District of Tennessee's includes the following cautionary message: "It is expected by the Court, however, that counsel for both sides shall make every good faith effort to comply with the letter and spirit of this Rule." M.D. Tenn. R. 10(a)(2)(n).

III. State Court Policies for the Treatment of *Brady* Material

This section describes state court statutes, rules, orders, and procedures that codify the *Brady* rule or incorporate specific aspects of it, define *Brady* material and/or set the timing and conditions for its disclosure, impose any due diligence obligations on the government, and specify sanctions for the government's failure to comply with such disclosure procedures.

A. Research Methods

We identified within all fifty states and the District of Columbia the relevant statewide legal authority governing prosecutorial disclosure of information favorable to the defendant. We searched relevant databases in Westlaw and LEXIS, including state statutes, criminal procedure rules, state court rules governing criminal discovery, state constitutions, state court opinions, and state rules on professional conduct. For most states, we were able to locate a relevant state rule, order, or other legal authority when we used the following search terms in various combinations:

- "exculpatory evidence";
- "favorable evidence";
- "*Brady* material";
- "prosecution disclosure"; and
- "suppression of evidence."

If we were unable to locate a rule for a state, we reviewed state court opinions to determine if case law addressed or clarified the legal obligation regarding prosecutorial disclosure of information favorable to the defendant.

Our analyses and conclusions are based on our interpretation of the relevant authorities that we identified. We looked for relevant legal authority that contained clear and unequivocal language regarding the duty of the prosecutor to disclose information to the defense. Where we could not identify authority with clear language regarding the prosecution's disclosure obligation, we erred on the side of caution and noted the absence of a clear authority regarding the duty to disclose.

B. Governing Rules, Orders, and Procedures

All fifty states and the District of Columbia address the prosecutor's obligation to disclose information favorable to the defendant. Table 3 shows the sources of the relevant authority.

Table 3. Sources of Authority for Prosecutor's Obligation to Disclose Evidence Favorable to the Defendant

Authorities[70]	Number of States	States
Rules of Criminal Procedure or general court rules	35	Ala., Alaska, Ariz., Ark., Colo., Del., D.C., Fla., Idaho, Ill., Ind., Iowa, Ky., Me., Md., Mass., Mich., Minn., Miss., Mo., N.H., N.J., N.M., N.D., Ohio, Pa., R.I., S.C., Tenn., Utah, Vt., Va., Wash., W. Va., Wyo.
General statutes	14	Conn., Ga., Kan., La., Mont., Neb., Nev., N.Y., N.C., Okla., Or., S.D., Tex., Wis.
Penal code	2	Cal., Haw.

Some state supreme courts have found prosecutors' suppression of exculpatory evidence to violate the due process clauses of their constitutions. For example, in *State v. Hatfield,* the West Virginia Supreme Court held that "[a] prosecution that withholds evidence which if made available would tend to exculpate an accused by creating a reasonable doubt as to his guilt violates due process of law under Article III, Section 14 of the West Virginia Constitution."[71] Another state, Nevada, explicitly notes in its criminal discovery procedure statute that "[t]he provisions of this section are not intended to affect any obligation placed upon the prosecuting attorney by the constitution of this state . . . to disclose exculpatory evidence to the defendant."[72]

C. Definition of *Brady* Material

In thirty-three of the fifty-one jurisdictions, we found rules or procedures that codify the *Brady* rule. There are differences in the *Brady*-related definitions of materials covered.

1. *Evidence favorable to the defendant*

Although there is some variation in the specific language used to define *Brady* material,[73] twenty-three states[74] have adopted language generally resembling the

---

70. We identified several states that address the favorable evidence disclosure obligation in more than one source, e.g., in a statute as well as in a rule. We charted only the highest authority.
71. 286 S.E.2d 402, 411 (W. Va. 1982).
72. Nev. Rev. Stat. § 174.235(3) (2004).
73. *See, e.g.,* Me. R. Crim. P. 16(a)(1)(C) ("any matter or information known to the attorney for the state which may not be known to the defendant and which tends to create a reasonable doubt of the defendant's guilt as to the offense charged.").

following: "any material or information which tends to negate the guilt of the accused as to the offense charged or would tend to reduce the accused's punishment therefor."[75]

2. *Exculpatory evidence or material*

Ten other states[76] expressly list exculpatory material as items of information that prosecutors are required to disclose. These states describe exculpatory material in two ways: as "exculpatory evidence"[77] or as "exculpatory material."[78]

The remaining states do not appear to have any express language regarding *Brady* material, but case law in several of those states discusses the *Brady* obligation. For example, in *Potts v. State*, the Georgia Supreme Court held that the "[d]efendant . . . has the burden of showing that the evidence withheld from him so impaired his defense that he was denied a fair trial within the meaning of the *Brady* Rule."[79] The Supreme Court of Wyoming noted that although "[t]here is no general constitutional right to discovery in a criminal case. . . . [s]uppression of evidence favorable to an accused upon request violates due process where the evidence is material to guilt."[80] Other state courts have similarly invoked the *Brady* rule in their decisions.[81]

No state procedure expressly refers to impeaching evidence as material subject to disclosure requirements, but three states specify that prosecutors must turn over any information required to be produced under the Due Process Clause of the U.S. Constitution.[82] Two states require disclosure pursuant to the *Brady* decision.[83] Despite this lack of express language, however, it appears that any state court

---

74. Ala., Ariz., Ark., Colo., Fla., Haw., Idaho, Ill., Ky., La., Me., Md., Minn., Mo., Mont., N.J., N.M., Ohio, Okla., Pa., Tex., Utah, and Wash.

75. Idaho Crim. R. 16(a).

76. Cal., Conn., Mass., Mich., Miss., Nev., N.H., Tenn., Vt., Wis.

77. *See, e.g.,* Nev. Rev. Stat. § 174.235(3).

78. *See, e.g.,* Cal. Penal Code § 1054.1(e).

79. 243 S.E.2d 510, 517 (Ga. 1978) (citation omitted).

80. Dodge v. State, 562 P.2d 303, 307 (Wyo. 1977) (citations omitted).

81. Bui v. State, 717 So. 2d 6, 27 (Ala. Crim. App. 1997) ("In order to prove a *Brady* violation, a defendant must show (1) that the prosecution suppressed evidence, (2) that the evidence was of a character favorable to his defense, and (3) that the evidence was material." (citation omitted)); O'Neil v. State, 691 A.2d 50, 54 (Del. 1997) ("[T]he [prosecution's] obligation to disclose exculpatory information is triggered by the defendant's request pursuant to Super. Ct. Crim. Rule 16 and is not limited to trial proceedings."); Lomax v. Commonwealth, 319 S.E.2d 763, 766 (Va. 1984) ("[T]he Commonwealth has a duty to disclose the [*Brady*] materials in sufficient time to afford an accused an opportunity to assess and develop the evidence for trial.").

82. *See, e.g.,* Nev. Rev. Stat. § 174.235(3); N.M. Dist. Ct. R. Cr. P. 5-501(A)(6); N.Y. Consol. Law Serv. Crim. P. Law § 240.20(1)(h).

83. *See, e.g.,* N.H. Super. Ct. R. 98(A)(2)(iv); Tenn. Crim. P. R. 16 (Advisory Commission Comments).

opinion that cites the *Brady* rule would include impeachment evidence as material that state prosecutors are constitutionally obliged to produce for defendants.[84]

D. Disclosure Requirements

Five states[85] use the term "favorable" in describing evidence subject to the state disclosure obligation. However, these states limit the clause "evidence favorable to the accused" with a condition that such evidence be "material and relevant to the issue of guilt or punishment."[86]

Although *Brady* used "favorable" in describing the evidence required for prosecutorial disclosure,[87] Rule 16 does not expressly refer to "favorable evidence." The rule permits a defendant in federal criminal cases to receive, upon request, documents and tangible objects within the possession of the government that *"are material to the preparation of the defendant's defense* or are intended for use by the government as evidence in chief at the trial, or were obtained from or belong to the defendant."[88] In describing some of the items of evidence subject to the criminal discovery right, twenty-six states use language identical or substantially similar to the italicized language above.[89]

1. *Types of information required to be disclosed*

All of the states,[90] require, at a minimum, disclosure of the types of evidence that Rule 16 permits to be disclosed before trial:

- written or recorded statements, admissions, or confessions made by the defendant;
- books, papers, documents, or tangible objects obtained from the defendant;

---

84. *See* United States v. Bagley, 473 U.S. 667, 676 ("Impeachment evidence, as well as exculpatory evidence, falls within the *Brady* rule.").

85. La., N.M., Ohio, Okla., Pa.

86. *See, e.g.,* Pa. R. Crim. P. 573 (B)(1)(a) ("The Commonwealth shall . . . permit the defendant's attorney to inspect and copy or photograph . . . any evidence favorable to the accused that is material either to guilt or to punishment."); La. Code Crim. P. Ann. art. 718 ("[O]n motion of the defendant, the court shall order the district attorney to permit or authorize the defendant to inspect, copy, examine . . . [evidence] favorable to the defendant and which [is] material and relevant to the issue of guilt or punishment.").

87. 373 U.S. at 87 ("[S]uppression by the prosecution of evidence favorable to an accused upon request violates due process where the evidence is material either to guilt or punishment.").

88. Fed. R. Crim. P. 16(a)(1)(C) (emphasis added).

89. Ala., Conn., Del., D.C., Haw., Idaho, Ind., Iowa, Kan., Ky., Miss., Mo., Neb., N.D., Ohio, Pa., S.C., S.D., Tenn., Tex., Utah, Vt., Va., Wash., W. Va., Wyo.

90. Indiana is unique in that it does not contain a separate rule for criminal discovery and relies on civil trial procedural rules to govern criminal trials. *See* Ind. Crim. R. 21 ("The Indiana rules of trial and appellate procedure shall apply to all criminal proceedings.") Therefore, Indiana does not provide a specific list of evidence subject to criminal discovery. Presumably, however, a criminal defendant in Indiana state court would be entitled to the basic items of evidence listed here.

- reports of experts in connection with results of any physical or mental examinations made of the defendant, and scientific tests or experiments made;
- records of the defendant's prior criminal convictions; and
- written lists of the names and addresses of persons having knowledge of relevant facts who may be called by the state as witnesses at trial.[91]

Some states, however, go beyond this basic list of information and specify other material for disclosure:

- any electronic surveillance of any conversations to which the defendant was a party;[92]
- whether an investigative subpoena has been executed in the case;[93]
- whether the case has involved an informant;[94]
- whether a search warrant has been executed in connection with the case;[95]
- transcripts of grand jury testimony relating to the case given by the defendant, or by a codefendant to be tried jointly;[96]
- police, arrest, and crime or offense reports;[97]
- felony convictions of any material witness whose credibility is likely to be critical to the outcome of the trial;[98]
- all promises, rewards, or inducements made to witnesses the state intends to present at trial;[99]
- DNA laboratory reports revealing a match to the defendant's DNA;[100]
- expert witnesses whom the prosecution will call at the hearing or trial, the subject of their testimony, and any reports they have submitted to the prosecution;[101]
- any information that indicates entrapment of the defendant;[102] and
- "any other evidence specifically identified by the defendant, provided the defendant can additionally establish that its disclosure would be in the interests of justice."[103]

---

91. *See, e.g.,* Conn. Gen. Stat. § 54-86(a) (2003); Idaho Crim. Rule 16(a).
92. Mont. Code Ann. § 415-15-322 (2)(a).
93. Mont. Code Ann. § 415-15-322 (2)(b).
94. Mont. Code Ann. § 415-15-322 (2)(c).
95. Ariz. St. RCRP R. 15.1(b)(10).
96. N.Y. Consol. Law Serv. Crim. P. Law § 240.20(1)(b).
97. Colo. Crim. P. Rule 16 (a)(I).
98. Cal. Penal Code § 1054.1(d).
99. Mass. Crim. P. R. 14(1)(A)(ix) (as amended, effective Sept. 7, 2004).
100. N.C. Gen. Stat. § 15A-903(g).
101. Wash. Super. Ct. Crim. R. 4.7(a)(2)(ii).
102. Wash. Super. Ct. Crim. R. 4.7(a)(2)(iii).
103. Pa. R. Crim. P. 573(B)(2)(a)(iv).

Most states provide that this "favorable" evidence *may* be disclosed to the defendant upon request or at the discretion of the court. Other states require that evidence beyond the scope of *Brady* material *must* be disclosed even without a request or court order.

2. *Mandatory disclosure without request*

Thirteen states[104] require mandatory disclosure of information "favorable" to the defense, regardless of whether the defendant made a specific discovery request for the material. We determined that this disclosure is mandatory because of the use of the phrase "prosecutor *shall* disclose," and the lack of any conditional clause such as "upon defendant's request," or "at the court's discretion." For example, Massachusetts describes as being "mandatory discovery for the defendant" the following items of evidence:

(i) Any written or recorded statements, and the substance of any oral statements, made by the defendant or a co-defendant.

(ii) The grand jury minutes, and the written or recorded statements of a person who has testified before a grand jury.

(iii) Any facts of an exculpatory nature.

(iv) The names, addresses, and dates of birth of the Commonwealth's prospective witnesses other than law enforcement witnesses . . . .

(v) The names and business addresses of prospective law enforcement witnesses.

(vi) Intended expert opinion evidence, other than evidence that pertains to the defendant's criminal responsibility . . . .

(vii) Material and relevant police reports, photographs, tangible objects, all intended exhibits, reports of physical examinations of any person or of scientific tests or experiments, and statements of persons the Commonwealth intends to call as witnesses.

(viii) A summary of identification procedures, and all statements made in the presence of or by an identifying witness that are relevant to the issue of identity or to the fairness or accuracy of the identification procedures.

(ix) Disclosure of all promises, rewards or inducements made to witnesses the Commonwealth intends to present at trial.[105]

In contrast, Hawaii requires disclosure of evidence favorable to the defendant only if the defendant is charged with a felony.[106] In cases other than felonies, Hawaii permits a state court, at its discretion, to require disclosure of favorable evidence "[u]pon a showing of materiality and if the request is reasonable."[107]

Of the thirteen states that require disclosure of favorable evidence, three distinguish between information that is subject to mandatory disclosure and other

---

104. Alaska, Ariz., Cal., Colo., Fla., Haw., Me., Md., Mass., N.H., N.M., Or., Wash.

105. Mass. Crim. P. Rule 14 (as amended, effective Sept. 7, 2004).

106. Haw. R. Penal P. 16(a) ("[D]iscovery under this rule may be obtained in and is limited to cases in which the defendant is charged with a felony.")

107. Haw. R. Penal P. 16(d).

evidence that must be specifically requested by the defendant or ordered by the court. Maine requires prosecutors to disclose the following items:

1. Statements obtained as a result of a search and seizure, statements resulting from any confession or admission made by the defendant, statements relating to a lineup or voice identification of the defendant.
2. Any written or recorded statements made by the defendant.
3. Any statement that tends to create a reasonable doubt of the defendant's guilt as to the offense charged.[108]

Maine requires the defendant to make a written request to compel the disclosure of books, papers, documents, tangible objects, reports of experts made in connection with the case, and names and addresses of the witnesses whom the state intends to call in any proceeding.[109]

The other two states that distinguish between items of evidence that are subject to mandatory disclosure are Maryland[110] and Washington.[111]

3. *Disclosure upon request of defendant*

Thirty-eight states[112] require a defendant to request favorable information, sometimes in writing, before the prosecution's obligation to disclose is triggered.

Ten states[113] place an additional condition on the defense:

- the defendant must make "a showing [to the court] that the items sought may be material to the preparation of his defense and that the request is reasonable,"[114] or
- the defendant must show "good cause" for discovery of such information.[115]

It appears that these ten states permit disclosure of certain favorable evidence only at the discretion of the trial court, and only if the court finds that the defendant has met the burden of proof in making the discovery request.

4. *Time requirements for disclosure*

States vary considerably in their time requirements for disclosure of *Brady* material. Some specify a time by which the prosecution must disclose favorable information, while others rely upon undefined terms such as "timely disclosure" or "as

---

108. Me. R. Crim. P. 16(a)(1)(A)–(C).
109. Me. R. Crim. P. 16(b).
110. Md. Rule 4-263.
111. Wash. Super. Ct. Crim. R. 4.7.
112. Ala., Ark., Conn., Del., D.C., Ga., Idaho, Ill., Ind., Iowa, Kan., Ky., La., Mich., Minn., Miss., Mo., Mont., Neb., Nev., N.J., N.Y., N.C., N.D., Ohio, Okla., Pa., R.I., S.C., S.D., Tenn., Tex., Utah, Vt., Va., W. Va., Wis., Wyo.
113. Conn., Idaho, Ind., Minn., Mo., Neb., Pa., Tex., Va., Wash.
114. Conn. Gen. Stat. § 54-86(a).
115. Tex. Code Crim. Proc. art. 39.14 (2004).

soon as practicable." Ten states[116] have established two separate time limits—one for the period within which the defendant must file a discovery request for favorable information and another for the period within which the prosecution must disclose the information.[117]

For a small number of states,[118] we were unable to determine a specific timetable for disclosure of *Brady* material. Nonetheless, it is probable that these states impose a "timely" disclosure requirement that would not prejudice the defendant's right to a fair trial.

a. Specific time requirement

Twenty-eight states[119] have mandated specific time limits for prosecutorial disclosure of evidence favorable to the defendant. Table 4 summarizes these time requirements.

Table 4. States with Specific Time Limits for Prosecutorial Disclosure of Evidence Favorable to the Defendant

State	Authority	Time Requirement
Alabama	Ala. R. Cr. P. 16.1	Within 14 days after the request has been filed in court
Arizona	Ariz. St. R. Cr. P. 15.6(c)	Not later than 7 days prior to trial
California	Cal. Penal Code § 1054.7	Not later than 30 days prior to trial
Colorado	Colo. Cr. P. R. 16(b)	Not later than 20 days after filing of charges
Connecticut	Conn. Gen. Stat. § 54-86(c)	Not later than 30 days after defendant pleads not guilty
Delaware	Del. Super. Ct. Crim. R. 16(d)(3)(B)	Within 20 days after service of discovery request
Florida	Fla. R. Cr. P. 3.220(b)(1)	Within 15 days after service of discovery request
Georgia	Ga. Code Ann. § 17-16-4(a)(1)	Not later than 10 days prior to trial
Hawaii	Haw. R. Penal P. 16(e)(1)	Within 10 calendar days after arraignment and plea of the defendant

---

116. D.C., Idaho, Mo., Nev., N.Y., Ohio, Okla., R.I., Va., W. Va.

117. *See, e.g.,* Nev. Rev. Stat. § 174.285 (2004) ("A request . . . may be made only within 30 days after arraignment or at such reasonable later time as the court may permit. . . . A party shall comply with a request made . . . not less than 30 days before trial or at such reasonable later time as the court may permit.").

118. D.C., Iowa, Pa., S.D., Tenn., Tex., and Wyo.

119. Ala., Ariz., Cal., Colo., Conn., Del., Fla., Ga., Haw., Idaho, Ind., Kan., Me., Md., Mass., Mich., Minn., Mo., Nev., N.H., N.J., N.M., N.Y., Ohio, Okla., R.I., S.C., Wash.

State	Authority	Time Requirement
Idaho	Idaho Cr. R. 16 (e)(1)	Within 14 days after service of discovery request
Indiana	Ind. R. Trial P. 34(B)	Within 30 days after service of discovery request
Kansas	Kan. Stat. Ann. § 22-3212(f)	Within 20 days after arraignment
Maine	Me. R. Crim. P. 16(a)(3)	Within 10 days after arraignment
Maryland	Md. R. 4-263(e)	Within 25 days after appearance of counsel or first appearance of defendant before the court, whichever is earlier
Massachusetts	Mass. Crim. P. Rule 14(1)(A)	At or prior to the pretrial conference
Michigan	Mich. Ct. R. 6.201(F)	Within 7 days after service of discovery request
Minnesota	Minn. R. Crim. P. 9.03; Minn. Bd. of Judicial Stand. R. 9(e)	Within 60 days after service of discovery request; by the time of the omnibus hearing
Missouri	Mo. Sup. Ct. R. 25.02	Within 10 days after service of discovery request
Nevada	Nev. Rev. Stat. § 174.285	Not later than 30 days prior to trial
New Hampshire	N.H. Sup. Ct. R. 98(A)(2)	Within 30 days after defendant pleads not guilty
New Jersey	N.J. Ct. R. 3:13-3(b)	Not later than 28 days after the indictment
New Mexico	N.M. R. Crim. P. 5-501(A)	Within 10 days after arraignment
New York	N.Y. Consol. Law Serv. Crim. P. Law § 240.80(3)	Within 15 days after service of discovery request
Ohio	Ohio R. Crim. P. 16(F)	Within 21 days after arraignment or 7 days prior to trial, whichever is earlier
Oklahoma	Okla. Stat. § 2002(D)	Not later than 10 days prior to trial
Rhode Island	R.I. Super. R. Crim. P. 16(g)(1)	Within 15 days after service of discovery request
South Carolina	S.C. R. Crim. P. 5(a)(3)	Not later than 30 days after service of discovery request
Washington	Wash. Super. Ct. Crim. R. 4.7(a)(1)	No later than the omnibus hearing

b. Nonspecific, descriptive time frame

Eighteen states[120] provide nonspecific, descriptive time requirements for disclosure of *Brady* material. The terms used for these general time frames include the following:

- "timely disclosure";[121]
- "as soon as practicable";[122]
- "a reasonable time in advance of trial date";[123]
- "within a reasonable time";[124]
- "in time for the defendants to make effective use of the evidence";[125]
- "as soon as possible";[126]
- "as soon as reasonably possible";[127] and
- "within a reasonable time before trial."[128]

State case law may provide guidance on whether a particular disclosure has satisfied the "timely" disclosure requirement. In general, however, the state courts have interpreted "timely" or "as soon as possible" to mean that the prosecution must disclose information favorable to the defendant "within a sufficient time for its effective use" by the defendant in preparation for his or her defense.[129] State courts that have ruled on the issue of timing of disclosures have emphasized that any disclosure must not constitute "unfair surprise" to the defendant and must not prejudice the defendant's right to a fair trial.[130]

---

120. Alaska, Ark., Ill., Ky., La., Me., Miss., Mont., Neb., N.C., N.D., Ohio, Or., Utah, Vt., Va., W. Va., Wis.

121. *See, e.g.,* Alaska R. Prof. Conduct 3.8(d); La. R. Prof. Conduct 3.8(d).

122. *See, e.g.,* Ark. R. Crim. P. 17.2(a); Ill. Sup. Ct. R. 412(d).

123. *See, e.g.,* Ky. R. Crim. P. 7.24(4).

124. *See, e.g.,* Me. R. Crim. P. 16(a).

125. *See, e.g.,* State v. Taylor, 472 S.E.2d 596, 607 (N.C. 1996) ("[D]ue process and *Brady* are satisfied by the disclosure of the evidence at trial, so long as disclosure is made in time for the defendants to make effective use of the evidence." (citations omitted))

126. *See, e.g.,* Vt. R. Crim. P. 16(b).

127. *See, e.g.,* State v. Hager, 342 S.E.2d 281, 284 (W. Va. 1986) ("[W. Va. R. Crim. P.] 16 impliedly sanctions the use of newly discovered evidence at trial, so long as the evidence is disclosed to the defense as soon as reasonably possible.")

128. *See, e.g.,* Wis. Stat. § 971.23(1).

129. State v. Harris, 680 N.W.2d 737, 754–55 (Wis. 2004) ("We hold that in order for evidence to be disclosed 'within a reasonable time before trial' . . . it must be disclosed within a sufficient time for its effective use. Were it otherwise, the State could withhold all *Brady* evidence until the day of trial in the hope that the defendant would plead guilty under the false assumption that no such evidence existed.").

130. State v. Golder, 9 P.3d 635 (Mont. 2000) (defendant argued that the timing of the state's formal disclosure of the two witnesses and the nature of their testimony constituted unfair surprise and jeopardized his right to a fair trial as assured under the Montana Constitution).

E. Due Diligence Obligations

By various means each state imposes a continuing duty on the prosecutor to locate and disclose additional favorable information discovered throughout the course of a trial. Delaware's Superior Court Rule 16(c) is typical of the rules in most states with a due diligence obligation:

> If, prior to or during trial, a party discovers additional evidence or material previously requested or ordered, which is subject to discovery or inspection under this rule, such party shall promptly notify the other party or that other party's attorney or the court of the existence of the additional evidence or material.[131]

Beyond this basic duty to supplement discovery of information, five states[132] require prosecutors to certify, in writing, that they have exercised diligent, good faith efforts in locating all favorable information, and that what has been disclosed is accurate and complete to the best of their knowledge or belief. For example, Florida requires the following:

> Every request for discovery or response . . . shall be signed by at least 1 attorney of record . . . [certifying] that . . . to the best of the signer's knowledge, information, or belief formed after a reasonable inquiry it is consistent with these rules and warranted by existing law . . . .[133]

Similarly, Massachusetts provides:

> When a party has provided all discovery required by this rule or by court order, it shall file with the court a Certificate of Compliance. The certificate shall state that, to the best of its knowledge and after reasonable inquiry, the party has disclosed and made available all items subject to discovery other than reports of experts, and shall identify each item provided.[134]

F. Sanctions for Noncompliance with *Brady* Obligations

All states provide remedies for prosecutorial nondisclosure that follow closely, if not explicitly mirror, Federal Rule of Criminal Procedure 16(d)(2), which states that a "court may order [the prosecution] to permit the discovery or inspection, grant a continuance, or prohibit [the prosecution] from introducing evidence not disclosed, or it may enter such other order as it deems just under the circumstances."[135]

In addition, eleven states[136] indicate that willful violations of a criminal discovery rule or court order requiring disclosure may subject the prosecution to other sanctions as the court deems appropriate. These sanctions "may include, but

---

131. Del. Super. Ct. R. 16(c).
132. Colo., Fla., Idaho, Mass., N.M.
133. Fla. R. Crim. P. 3.220(n)(3). *See also* Idaho Crim. R. 16(e) (Certificate of Service).
134. Mass. Crim. P. R. 14(a)(1)(E)(3) (as amended, effective Sept. 7, 2004).
135. Fed. R. Crim. P. 16(d)(2).
136. Ala., Ark., Fla., Haw., Ill., La., Minn., Mo., N.M., Vt., Wash.

are not limited to, contempt proceedings against the attorney . . . as well as the assessment of costs incurred by the opposing party, when appropriate."[137]

At least one state, Idaho, expressly states that failure to comply with the time prescribed for disclosure "shall be grounds for the imposition of sanctions by the court."[138] Other states probably also permit their courts to impose sanctions for failure to meet time requirements, as their rules provide remedies for failure to comply with *any* discovery rules, which can and often do include a time-limits provision.

At least three states[139] allow the court to order a dismissal as a possible sanction for particularly egregious violations of disclosure obligations. For example, Maine's rules state the following:

> If the attorney for the state fails to comply with this rule, the court on motion of the defendant or on its own motion may take appropriate action, which may include, but is not limited to, one or more of the following: requiring the attorney for the state to comply, granting the defendant additional time or a continuance . . . prohibiting the attorney for the state from introducing specified evidence and *dismissing charges with prejudice*.[140]

However, three states[141] regard dismissal to be too severe a sanction for nondisclosure. Louisiana's Code of Criminal Procedure notes that for disclosure violations, their state courts may "enter such other order, *other than dismissal*, as may be appropriate."[142] Similarly, the Supreme Court of Pennsylvania found dismissal to be "too severe" a sanction for failure to disclose *Brady* material, and explained that the discretion of Pennsylvania trial courts "is not unfettered."[143]

---

137. Fla. R. Crim. P. 3.220(n)(2).
138. Idaho Crim. Rule 16(e)(2).
139. Conn., Me., N.C.
140. Me. R. Crim. P. 16(d) (emphasis added).
141. La., Tex., Pa.
142. La. Code Crim. P. Ann. art. 729.5(A) (emphasis added).
143. Commonwealth v. Burke, 781 A.2d 1136, 1143 (Pa. 2001) ("[O]ur research has revealed [no judicial precedents] that approve or require a discharge as a remedy for a discovery violation. In fact, the precedents cited by the trial court and appellant support the view that the discharge ordered here was too severe . . . . [W]hile it is undoubtedly true that the trial court possesses some discretion in fashioning an appropriate remedy for a *Brady* violation, that discretion is not unfettered.").

www.ingramcontent.com/pod-product-compliance
Lightning Source LLC
Chambersburg PA
CBHW080528190526
45169CB00008B/3096